Embroidery Stitch Guide

With clear instructions and step-by-step diagrams for 58 beautiful embroidery stitches, this book is a treasure trove for beginners or stitchers who need a refresher course. It begins with a general explanation of the supplies you need and gives tips for stitching and finishing your projects. Then each stitch is shown individually in a full-color photo accompanied by how-to illustrations and instructions. The Heart Wreath on the front cover is an example of the endless creations you can make with this big collection of stitches. Happy stitching!

TABLE OF CONTENTS

General Directions 2
Arrowhead Stitch 4
Backstitch 4
Backstitch - Split 5
Backstitch - Threaded 5
Backstitch - Wrapped 6
Blanket Stitch 6
Blanket Stitch - Closed 7
Blanket Stitch - Double 7
Blanket Stitch - Looped 8
Blanket Stitch - Uneven 8
Blanket Stitch - Up and Down 9
Bullion Knot 9
Buttonhole Stitch 10
Buttonhole Stitch - Circular 10
Buttonhole Stitch - Scalloped 11
Chain Stitch 11
Chain Stitch - Braided 12
Chain Stitch - Cable 12
Chain Stitch - Open 13

Chain Stitch - Raised Band 13
Chain Stitch - Rosette 14
Chain Stitch - Twisted 14
Chain Stitch - Zigzag 15
Chevron Stitch 15
Colonial Knot 16
Coral Stitch 16
Coral Stitch - Zigzag 17
Cretan Stitch 17
Cross Stitch 18
Cross Stitch - Smyrna 18
Cross Stitch - Tied 19
Couching 19
Double Knot 20
Eyelet Stitch 20
Feather Stitch 21
Feather Stitch - Chained 21
Feather Stitch - Closed 22
Feather Stitch - Knotted 22
Fishbone Stitch 23

Fly Stitch 23
French Knot 24
Herringbone Stitch 24
Herringbone Stitch - Tied 25
Interlaced Band 25
Lazy Daisy Stitch 26
Loop Stitch 26
Maidenhair Stitch 27
Pekinese Stitch 27
Pistil Stitch 28
Satin Stitch 28
Scroll Stitch 29
Snail's Trail Stitch 29
Spider Web Stitch 30
Stem Stitch 30
Stem Stitch - Rosette 31
Turkey Work 31
Vandyke Stitch 32
Wheat Ear Stitch 32
Heart Wreath Pattern 33

LEISURE ARTS, INC.
Maumelle, Arkansas

Produced by

Production Team

Creative Directors: Jean Leinhauser and
Rita Weiss

Photographer: Carol Wilson Mansfield

Book Design: Linda Causee

Published by:

the art of everyday living

© 2013 by Leisure Arts, Inc.

104 Champs Blvd., STE. 100

Maumelle, AR 72113

www.leisurearts.com

General Directions

Embroidery Supplies

FABRICS

Almost any fabric can be used for embroidery: linen, cotton, silk, wool, synthetics, velvet, felt, terrycloth, twill, plain weaves or even weaves. Your project and personal taste will determine the fabric to use for your stitching.

When preparing fabric for embroidery, be sure to cut a large enough piece for your finished project, including extra that you might need for sewing seams or mounting on stretcher bars for hanging. Overcast or machine zigzag the raw edges of any fabric to prevent raveling.

NEEDLES

There are two types of needles that are used for embroidery. Sharps have a sharp point and tapestry needles have a blunt point. There are several types of Sharps called embroidery, crewel, and sewing, and are used for surface embroidery. Tapestry needles are used with evenweave fabrics, especially for counted cross stitch and needlepoint.

Needles are sized by number: the ones with the higher number are the smaller, thinner needles. Choose a needle size that is comfortable for you to work with. It should be easy to thread with the amount and size thread you are using. Be sure that your needle is not so large that it will leave holes in your fabric.

THREADS

There are several different threads on the market that can be used for embroidery, but the favorite is 6-strand cotton floss. It has a huge variety of colors to choose from and it can be separated so you can work with one strand, two strands or even three or more.

When preparing threads, cut into 18" lengths or a length with which you are comfortable working.

Hint: *If you are using several colors for a project, thread several needles in advance so they will be ready when you need to change colors.*

HOOPS AND FRAMES

The use of a hoop or frame is optional. Try some practice stitches with and without a hoop or frame and see what is comfortable for you. The most popular types of hoops are plastic or wood with a screw-type tension adjuster. If you use a hoop, try not to crush the stitched area as you progress and remove the hoop when you are not stitching.

For a larger project, a frame will hold your fabric taut throughout your stitching and help produce smooth, even stitching without distortion of your background fabric. There are several types of frames available on the market: plastic, snap-together frames, scroll-type wooden frames, or stretcher bars.

Getting Started

To begin stitching where there is no previous stitching, hold an inch of the thread end against the back of your fabric and anchor it with your first few stitches.

Another way to begin stitching is using a Waste Knot. Make a knot at the end of your thread and stitch down into the right side of your fabric a short distance ahead of your first few stitches (1). This waste knot will be on the front surface of your project.

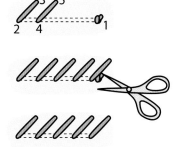

Bring your needle up at 2 and work a few stitches, anchoring the thread on the back of your fabric as you stitch. When you reach the knot, cut it off.

You can also use an Away Waste Knot to start your project. Make a knot at the end of your thread and stitch down into the right side of your fabric about 2 or 3 inches from your first stitch. This waste knot will be on the front surface of your project. Work your stitches, then cut off the waste knot. Thread the beginning thread into a needle and weave it

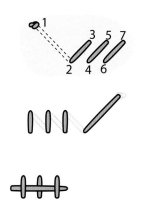

through your stitching on the back of your fabric.

Hint: *Be sure to only cut the waste knot. You will need the thread length to weave into the back of your stitches.*

To finish threads and begin new ones next to previous stitching, weave thread through the back of several stitches through like colors whenever possible. **Hint:** *Avoid carrying your threads across the back as it may show through to the front of your project.*

Stitching Tips and Techniques

When working with floss, always separate the strands then put together the number of strands you wish to use.

If a needle is difficult to thread, turn it over so you are threading the opposite side of the hole.

If you will be working with several colors and types of threads, thread each into a needle before beginning your first stitch. Each new color will be ready to use when you need it.

The neatest stitches are achieved by pulling the needle and thread completely through the fabric for each portion of the stitch.

Strive for consistent tension as you work. Practice any new stitches on a scrap fabric before stitching your project. If a mistake is made, remove the needle from the thread and unpick the work back to the error and restitch. If you try to unstitch your work, you will usually make a mess.

Finishing Notes

Dampen your embroidery project and place it face down on a clean dry towel or padded surface; press carefully until dry.

Hint: *Press iron onto embroidery; lift iron and move to next section. Continue lifting and pressing until project is dry. Do not move iron across fabric as it may become distorted.*

Mount your stitched piece onto stretcher bars and frame as desired. If you would like a slightly puffed look, add a layer of fleece beneath the embroidery.

Arrowhead Stitch

The Arrowhead Stitch is worked between two imaginary parallel lines. Bring thread up at 1 and stitch down at 2, making a diagonal stitch. Come up at 3 and down at 4, making a diagonal stitch in the opposite direction. Continue in this manner until you achieve the desired length.

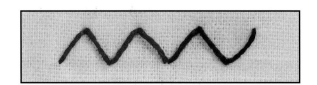

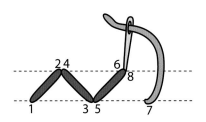

Backstitch

Bring the needle up at 1, a stitch length away from beginning of design line. Stitch back down at 2, at the beginning of the line. Bring your needle up at 3 then stitch back down to meet previous stitch at 1.

Continue in this manner, stitching backward on surface to meet previous stitch. Backstitches can be worked along curved or straight lines.

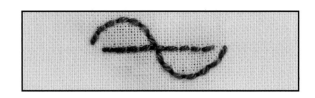

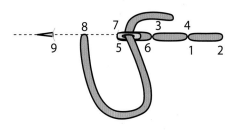

Backstitch - Split

Begin as for Backstitch (page 4), up at 1, down at 2, and up at 3. Stitch down at 4, this time splitting the thread of the first stitch, and come up at 5. Continue in this manner, each time splitting the previous stitch.

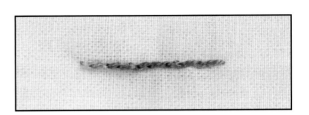

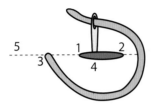

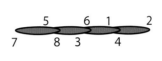

Backstitch - Threaded

Work a row of Backstitches (page 4).

Bring a matching or contrasting thread up at A, at beginning of line. Pass the needle upward beneath first Backstitch, not entering the fabric. Pull through, leaving a loose loop below the Backstitch.

Pass needle downward in same manner beneath second Backstitch. Repeat to the end of the Backstitch line and stitch down into fabric at B. Keep the loops consistent above and below backstitched line.

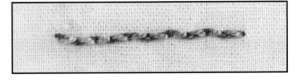

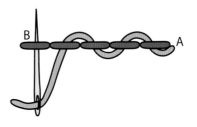

Backstitch - Wrapped

Work a row of Backstitches (page 4).

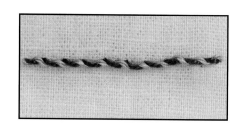

Using a matching or contrasting thread, bring needle up at A, at beginning of line. Use an overcasting motion, pass needle downward beneath each Backstitch. Be sure not to stitch into the fabric.

Pull through consistently so each Backstitch is loosely wrapped. Stitch down into fabric at end of backstitched line at B.

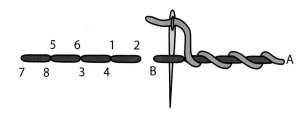

Blanket Stitch

Bring the needle up at 1 and reinsert needle at 2 (diagonally to the right of 1). Bring needle up at 3 (down and slightly to left of 2) keeping the thread under the point of the needle.

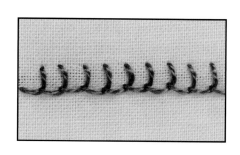

Pull thread through to form stitch. Continue working from left to right keeping stitches the same distance apart and the same height.

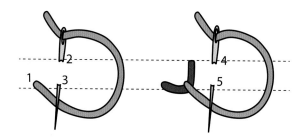
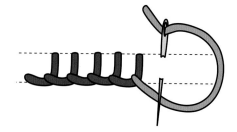

Blanket Stitch - Closed

The Closed Blanket Stitch is similar to the regular Blanket Stitch except that the tops of the stitches are worked into the same hole (2) to form a triangular shape.

Bring the needle up at 1. Loop thread to the right and insert needle at 2. Bring needle back up at 3, making sure needle goes over the thread and pull into place. Go down at 4 (same hole as 2) and come up at 5 to form the triangle. Continue in same manner, working left to right.

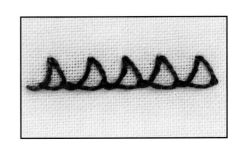

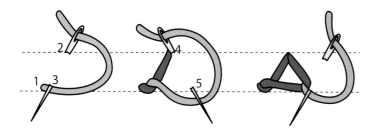

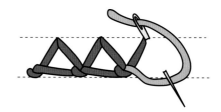

Blanket Stitch - Double

Work two rows of Blanket Stitch so they mesh together with straight edges along the outer sides.

Work one row of Blanket Stitches (page 6).

Turn fabric upside down and work a second row in between the stitches of the first row but not quite touching. If desired, different colors may be used for each row.

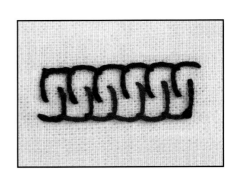

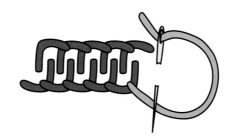

Blanket Stitch - Looped

Bring thread up at 1 and loop thread counterclockwise. Stitch down at 2 and up at 3 with thread beneath point of needle; pull through. Stitch down at 4 to anchor loop and up at 5 (within loop). Repeat sequence for desired length.

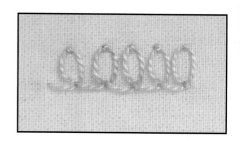

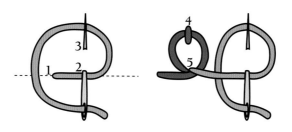

Blanket Stitch - Uneven

Begin this stitch the same as the regular Blanket Stitch (page 6).

Come up at 1, down at 2; holding thread with thumb of non-stitching hand, emerge at 3 (slightly to left of 2 and slightly above 1). For the second stitch, go down at 4 (above 2) and emerge at 5. Continue in same manner adjusting height of each stitch as desired.

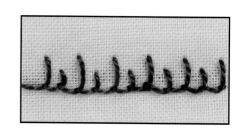

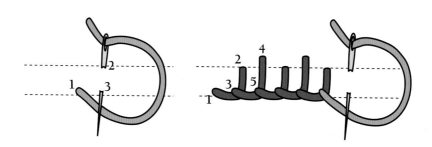

Blanket Stitch - Up and Down

Bring the needle up at 1; hold thread down with thumb of non-stitching hand. Go down at 2 and bring up at 3 keeping tip of needle over the thread. Go down at 4 (next to, but not in 3) and emerge at 5 (next to, but not in 2). Pull thread down until stitch is formed.

Continue in same manner starting by working left to right going down at 6, up at 7 with needle tip over the looped thread.

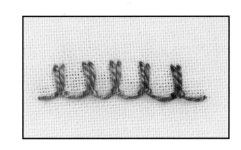

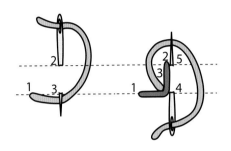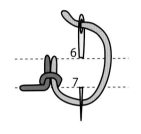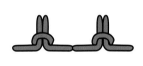

Bullion Knot

Come up at 1, pulling needle completely through. Go down at 2 and re-emerge at 1; do not pull needle all the way through fabric.

Wrap thread around top of needle 5 or 6 times (or until length of twists equals the space between 1 and 2).

Pull needle through, holding twists with other hand, close to fabric. Go down at 2, pulling firmly to shape knot.

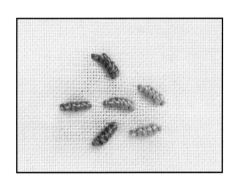

Buttonhole Stitch

Work Buttonhole stitch the same as for the Blanket Stitch (page 6); make stitches close together to fill an area.

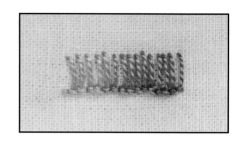

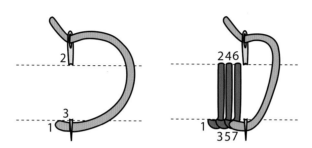

Buttonhole Stitch - Circular

Work Buttonhole Stitches around a central hole of fabric. Begin as for Buttonhole Stitch (above), coming up at 1, down at 2 (center), up at 3 with loop underneath tip of needle and pull through.

Working counterclockwise, make additional stitches, always entering fabric at center and coming out along the outside edge. To end, stitch down over final loop into same hole as 3.

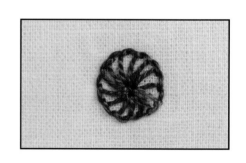

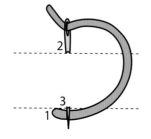

Buttonhole Stitch - Scalloped

Work Buttonhole Stitch (page 10), but increase the length of each stitch until it is the length you desire; then decrease the length of each stitch.

Continue in this manner to form a scallop pattern.

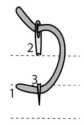 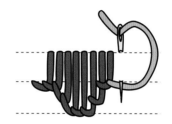

Chain Stitch

Bring needle up at 1, form a counter-clockwise loop and go down at 2 (same hole as 1), holding loop with left thumb. Come up at 3 bringing the tip of your needle over the loop. Repeat stitch to form a chain. The chain can be worked horizontally, vertically, or along a curve. End chain by making small stitch over final loop.

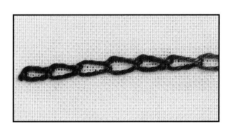

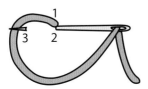 

Chain Stitch - Braided

Make a small stitch coming up at 1 and going down at 2; emerge at 3. Pass needle under small stitch from right to left and go down at 4 (same hole as 3); emerge at 5. Pass needle under original small stitch and go down at 6 (same hole as 5).

Emerge at 7, pass needle under first chain, and go down at 8 (same hole as 7). Continue in same manner working from top to bottom passing needle under the chain made before the previous chain.

Chain Stitch - Cable

Bring needle up at 1; wrap thread once around needle.

Go down at 2, pull snugly and emerge at 3 with tip of needle over thread.

Pull thread gently to complete stitch.

Continue in same manner working top to bottom.

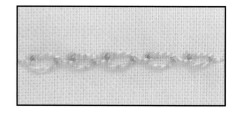

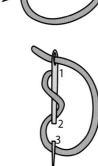 

Chain Stitch - Open

Come up at 1 and down at 2 (even with 1) forming a loop. Emerge at 3 (directly below 1) with needle tip over loop; leave loop loose.

Go down at 4 above loop (directly below 2 and to the right of 3) and emerge at 5. Pull thread to form stitch, leaving loop loose. Continue in same manner working from top to bottom along two imaginary lines.

Tack down last loop with two short stitches, A and B.

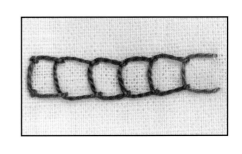

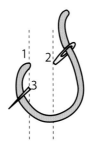 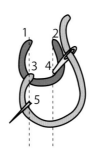 

Chain Stitch - Raised Band

Work the desired number of equal-length straight stitches that are spaced closely together. With another thread (the same or a contrasting color), come up at 1, pass needle under first straight stitch, toward the left of 1. Form a loop and coming from the top, pass needle under first Straight Stitch toward the right of 1, with needle tip above loop. Pull through to form knot. Continue stitching in same manner, ending by stitching down over last loop.

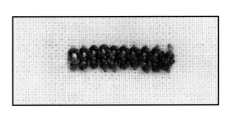

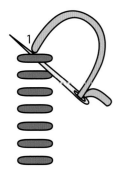  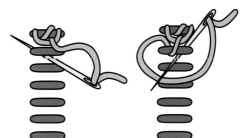 

Chain Stitch - Rosette

The Chain Stitch - Rosette is worked right to left.

Bring needle up at 1, form a counterclockwise loop, and go down at 2 (to the left of 1), emerge at 3 with tip of needle over loop. Pull needle through loop completely, but not too tightly.

For next stitch, pass needle under top right thread (to the left of 1); form loop and continue next stitch in same manner.

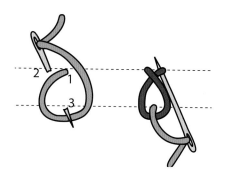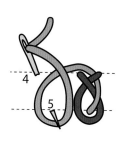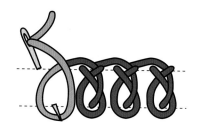

Chain Stitch - Twisted

Come up at 1 and form a counterclockwise loop; go down at 2 (to the left of 1) and up at 3 with loop beneath point of needle.

Stitch down at 4 (to the left of 3 and outside of first loop) and form a new counterclockwise loop; come up at 5. Continue in this manner; tack down final loop with a small straight stitch.

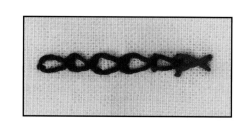

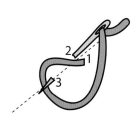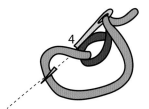

Chain Stitch - Zigzag

Come up at 1 and form a counterclockwise loop; go down at 2 (same hole as 1) and come back up at 3 (to left of and below 1). Be sure tip of needle is over loop.

Pull needle through completely and form another loop; go down at 4 (same hole as 3), piercing lower end of first loop. Come back up at 5 (to the left of and even with 1). Continue in same manner for length desired.

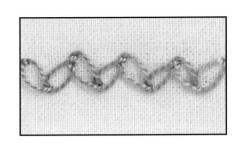

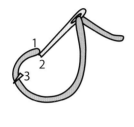  

Chevron Stitch

The Chevron Stitch is worked from left to right between two imaginary parallel design lines. It can be used as a border or filling. Bring needle up at 1 and down at 2; hold the thread down with thumb of non-stitching hand and make a small stitch bringing needle up at 3 (halfway between 1 and 2). Reinsert needle at 4, diagonally above 3, and bring out at 5. Insert your needle at 6 keeping thread above needle and bring out at 7 (same hole as 4). Insert at 8 and come up at 9. Continue working stitch in same manner.

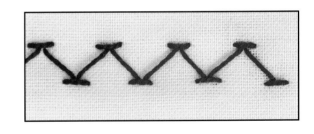

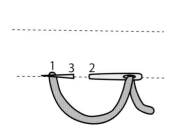 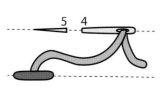 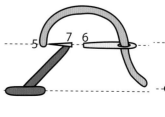 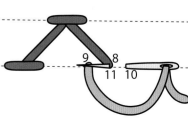

Colonial Knot

Come up at 1, make a clockwise loop and slip point of needle beneath thread from left to right. Bring thread around point of needle in a figure eight motion.

Insert needle at 2 (next to, but not into 1); pull thread while pulling needle through to back of fabric.

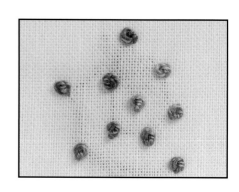

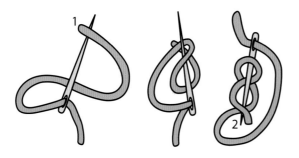

Coral Stitch

This stitch is made along an imaginary line, but can be worked in any direction or along a curve. Come up at 1 and make a counterclockwise loop, holding thread out toward the left.

Stitch down at 2 (outside of loop) and up at 3 (just below 2 and inside of loop),with loop beneath point of needle. Pull through. Repeat and stitch down at end to anchor final knot.

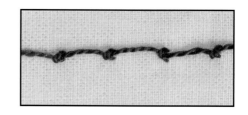

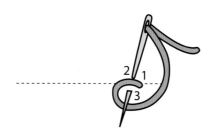

Coral Stitch - Zigzag

Work the Coral Zigzag Stitch from right to left between two imaginary parallel lines. Come up at 1, swing thread in a counterclockwise loop, and stitch down at 2, and up at 3; pull through to form first knot on upper line.

Hold thread in a similar position and stitch down at 4 diagonally downward from first knot, and bring needle out at 5; pull needle through.

Repeat on upper line and continue in a zigzag manner.

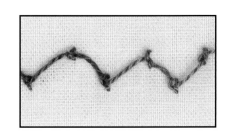

 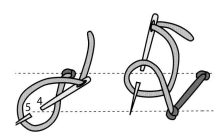 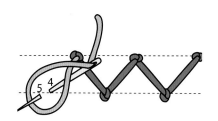

Cretan Stitch

Come up at 1. Go down at 2 (above and to the right of 1) and emerge at 3 (directly below and desired distance from 2) with tip of needle over top of thread.

Insert needle at 4 and emerge at 5 (directly above 4 and the same distance as between 2 and 3) with tip of needle over top of thread.

Continue working in same manner along pairs of imaginary parallel lines, keeping vertical stitches evenly spaced.

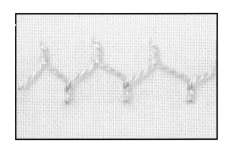

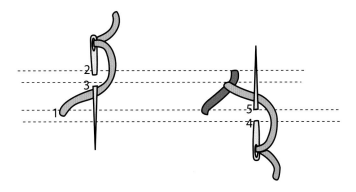

Cross Stitch

Bring needle up at 1 and down at 2. Complete the stitch by coming up at 3 and down at 4. When doing a row of Cross Stitches, make all stitches from 1 to 2 first, going from left to right.

Complete row by working from right to left along two imaginary parallel lines with stitches from bottom right to upper left.

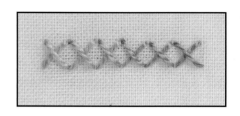

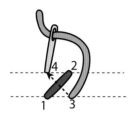 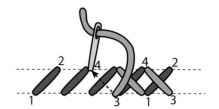

Cross Stitch - Smyrna

Begin as for Cross Stitch (above) making long stitches (1-2 and 3-4), then make a vertical stitch (5-6) and a horizontal stitch (7-8) to create a square shape. Work horizontal rows from left to right.

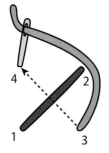 

Cross Stitch - Tied

Begin as for a Cross Stitch (page 18), coming up at 1, down at 2, up at 3 and down at 4. Work a center horizontal or vertical stitch by coming up at 5 and down at 6 to tie down the center of the stitch. Work rows from left to right.

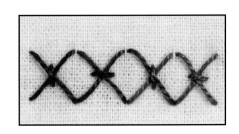

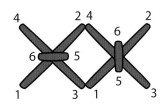

Couching

Work this stitch in any direction and along curves. Bring thread up at 1, the beginning of the design line, and park the thread temporarily out of the way.

Using a matching or contrasting thread, come up at A, down at B, up at C, etc., taking small stitches to hold the original thread in place. Stitch down at 2 to end couched thread.

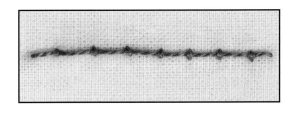

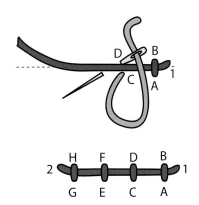

Double Knot

Come up at 1, go down at 2 (to the right of and below 1) and emerge at 3 (directly across from 2); pull needle through. Pass needle over top and under stitch just made; pull needle through.

Form counterclockwise loop and pass needle under beginning stitch and over loop. Pull thread to form knot. Continue with next stitch in same manner.

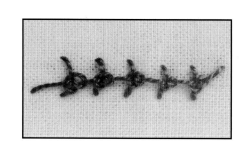

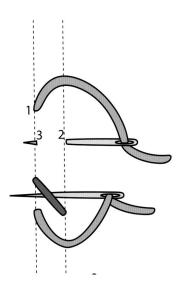
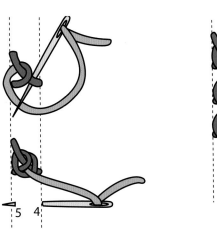

Eyelet Stitch

Bring thread up at 1; follow the arrow and stitch down at the center of the shape. Come up at 2, again on the outside, and stitch down at center.

Continue in this manner, working clockwise around the center, to fill the shape. If thread is slightly pulled after each downward stitch, a small hole will appear at the center of the Eyelet.

Feather Stitch

Come up at 1 and go down at 2 (to left of and even with 1); emerge at 3 (below and between 1 and 2) with tip of needle over thread.

Pull thread completely through and go down at 4; emerge at 5 (below 3 and 4 and directly under 1).

Pull thread completely through and continue stitching in same manner. End by making a small stitch over last loop.

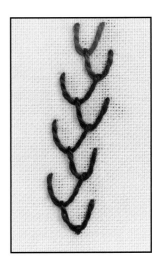

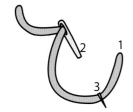

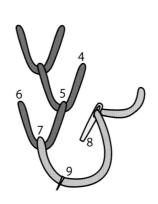

Feather Stitch - Chained

Begin stitch as for Chain Stitch (page 11). Come up at 1, loop thread and go down again at 2 (same hole as 1); emerge at 3 (below and to the left of 1), with tip of needle over thread. Pull thread through and go down at 4 making a slanted Straight Stitch. Come up at 5, form loop and go down at 6 (same hole as 5), emerging at 7 to form next chain. Go down at 8 making a slanted Straight Stitch. Continue in same manner forming a zigzag pattern with Straight Stitches.

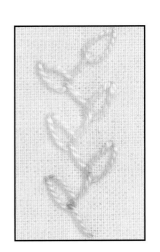

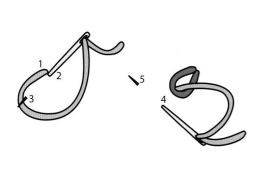

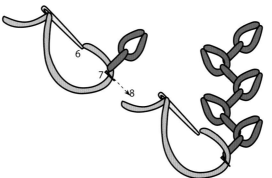

Feather Stitch - Closed

Come up at 1 and go down at 2 (to the right of and slightly above 1); emerge at 3 (directly below 2) with tip of needle over thread. Pull needle through completely and go down at 4 (next to and slightly below 1); emerge at 5 (directly below 4). Continue in same manner for desired length.

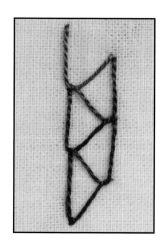

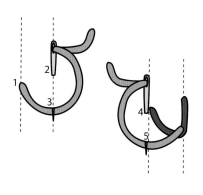 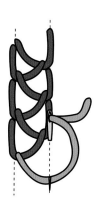

Feather Stitch - Knotted

Come up at 1, form a counterclockwise loop and go down at 2 (above and to the left of 1); emerge at 3 (below and slightly to the left of 2) with the tip of your needle over the thread. Pull needle through and form a clockwise loop; go down at 4 and emerge at 5 going through loop.

Pull needle through and form a counterclockwise loop; go down at 6 and emerge at 7 going through loop. Pull needle through and continue stitching in same manner.

Fishbone Stitch

This stitch can be used to fill in shapes such as leaves. Mark desired shape on fabric. Bring needle up at 1 and down the desired distance. Come back up at 2 (at outline of the drawn shape) and down over lower end of first stitch. Come up at 3 (at outline of the drawn shape) and down covering lower edge of previous stitch.

Continue in same manner alternating from side to side.

Fly Stitch

Bring the needle up at 1 and down at 2; keep stitch loose. Come up at 3 and pull thread to form a "V"; go down at 4. Continue in same manner going vertically or horizontally.

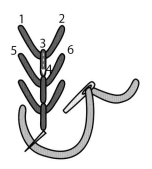

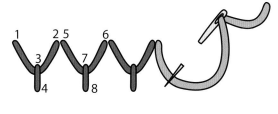

French Knot

Bring needle up at 1. Wrap thread once around shaft of needle. Insert point of needle at 2 (close to, but not into 1). Hold knot down as you pull the needle through to the back of fabric.

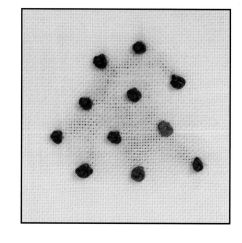

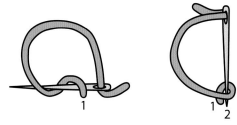

Herringbone Stitch

Bring needle up at 1 along an imaginary line. Insert needle at 2, diagonally above 1 and bring up at 3. Reinsert needle at 4 and bring out at 5. Continue in this manner working from left to right. This stitch can be used as a border or filler.

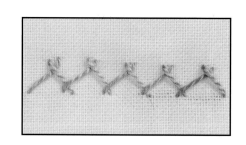

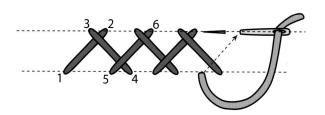

Herringbone Stitch - Tied

Bring needle up at 1 along an imaginary line. Insert needle at 2, diagonally above 1 and bring up at 3 (to the left of 2). Reinsert needle at 4 and bring out at 5. Continue in this manner working from left to right.

Using the same color or a contrasting thread, work short vertical stitches (coming up at A and going down at B) over each intersection.

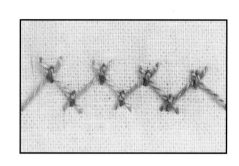

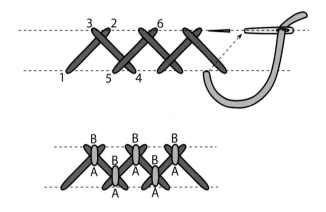

Interlaced Band

Work Interlaced Band between two imaginary lines.

Along each line, work a row of Backstitches (page 4). For first row, bring needle up at 1, a stitch length away from beginning of design line. Stitch back down at 2, at beginning of line. Bring needle up at 3 then stitch back down to meet previous stitch at 1. Continue in this manner, stitching backward on surface to meet previous stitch.

Stitch a second row of Backstitches below and slightly to the right of the top row.

Using the same or contrasting color, come up at A, loop over the first upper row Backstitch from front to back, then loop over and under the first lower row Backstitch. Continue in this manner until the end of the Backstitch rows; stitch down to end work.

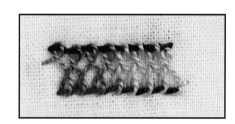

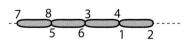

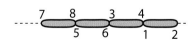

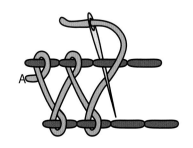

Lazy Daisy Stitch

Bring needle up at 1 and reinsert needle at 2 (same hole as 1). Pull thread until loop is desired length. Bring needle up at 3 (inside loop) and pull thread until loop is desired length. Stitch down over the loop at 4.

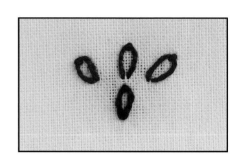

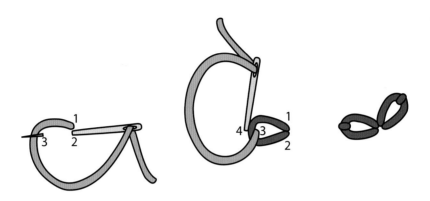

Loop Stitch

Come up at 1, go down at 2 (above and to the left of 1); come back up at 3 (directly below 2). Pass needle over and under first stitch and pull needle through with tip over top of thread to form knot. For next stitch go down at 4 and come up at 5.

Pass needle over and under stitch just made and pull through with tip of needle over top of thread. Continue in same manner for desired length.

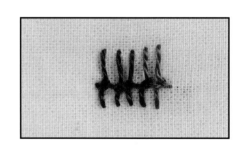

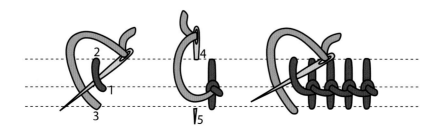

Maidenhair Stitch

Come up at 1 and down at 2 (to the left of and even with 1); emerge at 3 (below and to the left of 1) bringing tip of needle over thread. Pull needle through and go down at 4 (below and to the left of 2); emerge at 5 (below and to the left of 3). Pull needle through and go down at 6 (below and to the left of 4) and emerge at 7 (below and to left of 5).

Pull needle through and go down at 8 (to right and even with 7) and emerge at 9. Continue in same manner for two more stitches, then do alternating groups of three stitches for desired length.

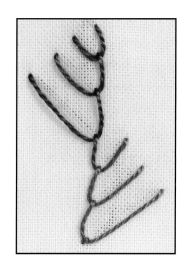

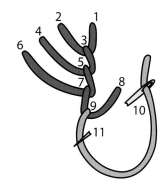

Pekinese Stitch

Make a row of small Backstitches (page 4). Using a thread of the same (or contrasting) color, come up at A and pass needle under second Backstitch from the left.

Loop thread counterclockwise and pass needle under first Backstitch with tip of needle over top of loop, leaving stitch loose. Continue looping stitches along entire Backstitch row.

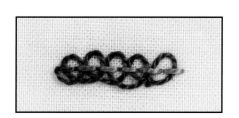

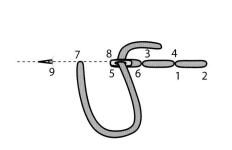

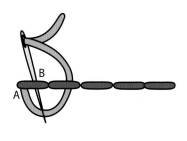

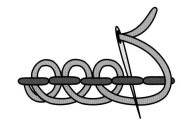

Pistil Stitch

Bring needle up at 1, wrap thread twice around shaft of needle. Swing point of needle clockwise and reinsert at 2, desired distance from 1. Pull wrapping thread around needle and hold with thumb and forefinger of non-stitching hand while pulling needle through to back of fabric.

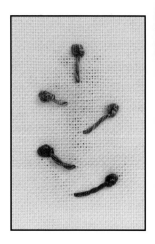

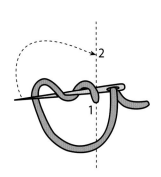 

Satin Stitch

Come up at 1 and down at 2. Continue with Straight Stitches very close together to fill desired pattern.

Use the Satin Stitch to fill any desired shape.

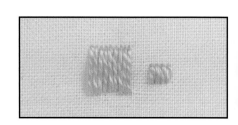

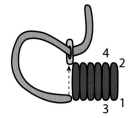

Scroll Stitch

Come up at 1. Loop thread clockwise to the right of 1; hold loop in place with thumb or non-stitching hand. Go down at 2 and up at 3 (to left of and below 2) making a small stitch inside of loop. Pull thread to tighten loop and pull needle through while holding tightened loop in place. Continue stitching left to right for desired length.

Snail's Trail Stitch

Come up at 1 and make a counterclockwise loop (to left of 1). Holding down loop with thumb of non-stitching hand go down at 2 (above and to left of 1) and emerge at 3 (to left of and even with 1) with tip of needle over loop. Pull needle through and continue stitching in same manner.

Spider Web Stitch

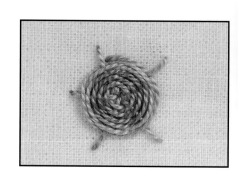

Begin the Spider Web by making a Fly Stitch (page 23). Bring the needle up at 1 and down at 2, keeping stitch loose. Come up at 3, pull thread to form a "V" and go down at 4.

Add two extra stitches to make a total of five spokes. Come up at 5 and down at 6, then up at 7 and down at 8.

Bring the same color or contrasting thread up at the center and begin weaving over and under the five spokes in a spiral manner until you reach desired fullness.

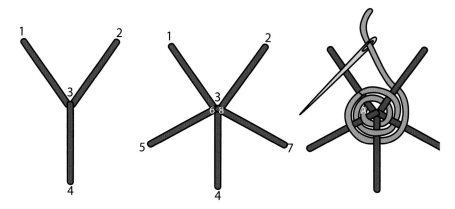

Stem Stitch

Bring needle up at 1. Hold thread down with the thumb of your non-stitching hand. Reinsert needle at 2 and bring up at 3, about halfway between 1 and 2. Pull the thread through and continue in this manner with thread held below stitching. Work in straight or curved lines.

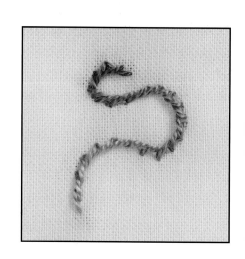

Stem Stitch - Rosette

Start with three Stem Stitches (page 30) for the center of the Rosette.

Bring the needle up at 1. Hold thread down with the thumb of your non-stitching hand. Reinsert needle at 2 and bring up at 3, about halfway between 1 and 2. Pull the thread through and continue in this manner with thread held below stitching.

Continue adding Stem Stitches circling outward until desired size is reached.

Turkey Work

Begin stitching on top of fabric. Stitch down at 1, leaving the thread end free; come up at 2 and pull through. Stitch down at 3 and up at 4 (same hole as 1); pull through.

Swing the thread above work, stitch down at 5 and up at 6 (same hole as 3); pull partially through, leaving a loop.

Stitch down at 7 and up at 8 being sure to go below loop just made; pull through to anchor loop.

Continue stitching in this manner until end of row is reached; stitch down to anchor last loop.

Begin next row below the first, working left to right. Repeat rows in this manner, keeping the loops toward the top and anchor stitches at the bottom.

You can leave the loops or cut for a fuzzy effect.

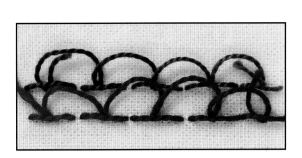

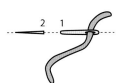
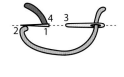

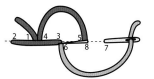

Vandyke Stitch

Come up at 1 and down at 2; come back up at 3 (to the left of and even with 2) and go down at 4. Come up at 5 (directly below and even with 1) and pass needle under area where threads cross, going from right to left. Pull needle through, keeping loop loose.

Go down at 6 (directly below and even with 4) and back up at 7 (directly below and even with 5). Pass needle under previous crossed stitches and go down at 8. Continue in same manner for desired length.

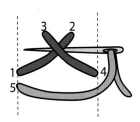 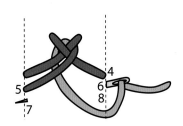

Wheat Ear Stitch

Come up at 1 and down at 2, up at 3 (even with and to the right of 1) and down at 4 (same hole as 2). Emerge at 5, directly below 2 and 4 (about same distance as the length between 1 and 2 and 3 and 4). Pull needle through completely and loop needle under the two stitches just made going from right to left. Go down at 6 (same hole as 5). Come back up at 7 and continue next stitch in same manner.

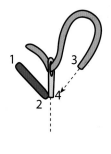 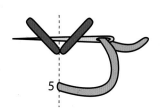 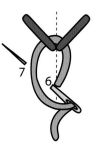